Jim Bridger: The Life and Legacy of Ameri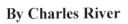

By Charles River

About Charles River Editors

Charles River Editors provides superior editing and original writing services across the digital publishing industry, with the expertise to create digital content for publishers across a vast range of subject matter. In addition to providing original digital content for third party publishers, we also republish civilization's greatest literary works, bringing them to new generations of readers via ebooks.

Sign up here to receive updates about free books as we publish them, and visit Our Kindle Author Page to browse today's free promotions and our most recently published Kindle titles.

Introduction

David Alan Clark's sculpture of Bridger in Wyoming

Jim Bridger

Exploration of the early American West, beginning with Lewis and Clark's transcontinental trek at the behest of President Thomas Jefferson, was not accomplished by standing armies, the era's new steam train technology, or by way of land grabs. These came later, but not until pathways known only to a few of the land's indigenous people were discovered, carved out, and charted in an area stretching from the eastern Rocky Mountains to the Pacific Ocean, and the present-day borders of Mexico and Canada. Even the great survey parties, such as Colonel William Powell's exploration of the Colorado River, came decades later. The first views of Western America's enormity by white Americans were seen by individuals of an entirely different personality, in an era that could only exist apart from its home civilization. The American mountain man, with his myriad of practical skills, could endure isolation in a way most could not. He lived in constant peril from the extremes of nature and from the hostilities of cultures unlike his own. In an emergency, assistance was rarely available, and he rarely stayed in one place long enough to build even a simple shelter. Travel in the American West relied upon a specific calendar, and to ignore it could be fatal, as many discovered, to their misfortune. Winter in the mountainous regions of the Rocky Mountains and Cascades was lethally cold to explorer and settler alike, but desert areas and grass plains presented difficulties as well. The network of rivers flowing west of the Mississippi on both sides of the continental divide served as early highways to the Wyoming and Montana regions, the Oregon Territory, Utah and Colorado, and the California southwest. Some were placidly tranquil, while others raged through the extreme elevations, all but defying navigation. Contact with indigenous tribes was problematic enough with linguistic and cultural barriers, but to survive, there required a sensitivity to tribal food sources and sacred areas when traveling. The profession of trapping was, in itself, a trespass on Native American resources, and yet the mountain man's existence was fueled, in part, by the tangible rewards of the fur trapping trade. Beaver hats were all the rage in Europe, and the market had to be satisfied by a group of courageous individualists. Apart from fashion, the beaver pelt provided a "warmth [and] luxurious texture,"[1] not found in other land animals. As American beaver pelts flooded European markets, North American companies–such as Hudson's Bay, the American Fur Company, the Rocky Mountain Fur Company, and Manuel Lisa's Missouri Fur Company—competed for Western resources thought to be limitless. The effort to acquire pelts was laborious and dangerous, but as long as the price per pound remained high, wealth awaited individuals committed to the rigors of the trade. Apart from such realities, the mountain man's poetically obsessive kinship with undiscovered lands and unspoiled nature, free from society's trappings, was secondary. The aesthetic aspect was a luxury to be enjoyed once work had been done and safety assured. Distant observers who heard or read of the journey were fascinated with the peripheral glamor, but not enamored of the work's grisly nature.

    A small group of individuals have come down to us as famous figures from the fur trapping

---

[1] A Brief History of the Beaver Trade – www.ucsc.edu/feinstein/A%20brief%2020of%20%20beaver%20trade.html

era of the 19th century, but explorer and guide Jim Bridger is the most distinguished of the lot. This is because he remained in a dangerous and vast Western wilderness long after the fur trade's demise in addition to powers of observation enabling him to create accurate maps decades after passing through any terrain. Blessed with a rare gift for mentally recording every landscape through which he passed in minute detail, many modern transportation routes have sprung from what was first etched in sand with the point of Bridger's stick, including major interstate highways and railroad lines. As a pathfinder, guide, and map-maker of uncanny accuracy despite the primitive nature of his easel, he personally escorted settlers, gold-seekers, religious bands, adventurers, and military expeditions into the West, venturing further into virgin territory as the expanding population encroached on his privacy.

Jim Bridger: The Life and Legacy of America's Most Famous Mountain Man examines the legendary career of the trapper, scout, guide, and soldier. Along with pictures of important people, places, and events, you will learn about Jim Bridger like never before.

Jim Bridger: The Life and Legacy of America's Most Famous Mountain Man

About Charles River Editors

Introduction

    The Louisiana Purchase

    Bridger's Early Years

    Early Expeditions

    Pushing West

    Conflicts

    Death and Legacy

    Online Resources

    Bibliography

The Louisiana Purchase

Throughout his presidency at the beginning of the 19th century, Thomas Jefferson had worried about the future of the western U.S., seeing that settlements in the Ohio Valley and lower South relied upon the Mississippi River. France's controls over the region, in his estimation, put the U.S. at a severe disadvantage. His solution proved successful beyond his wildest imagination, for Napoleon did not only sell New Orleans to the U.S, the portion that Jefferson instructed his ministers to make an offer on, but all of "New France," the entire area of Louisiana. Jefferson might have said later that his purchase of the territory "strained" but did not "break" the Constitution, but also should have boasted that, with one stroke, he had removed one less obstacle to American expansionism.

Jefferson

The Louisiana Purchase encompassed all or part of 15 current U.S. states and two Canadian provinces, including Arkansas, Missouri, Iowa, Oklahoma, Kansas, Nebraska, parts of Minnesota that were west of the Mississippi River, most of North Dakota, nearly all of South Dakota, northeastern New Mexico, Northern Texas, the portions of Montana, Wyoming, and Colorado east of the Continental Divide, and Louisiana west of the Mississippi River, including the city of New Orleans. (parts of this area were still claimed by Spain at the time of the Purchase.) In addition, the Purchase contained small portions of land that would eventually become part of the Canadian provinces of Alberta and Saskatchewan. The purchase, which doubled the size of the United States, comprises around 23% of current U.S. territory.

The purchase was a vital moment in Jefferson's presidency. At the time, it faced domestic opposition as being possibly unconstitutional, and though he felt that the U.S. Constitution did not contain any provisions for acquiring territory, Jefferson decided to purchase Louisiana because he felt uneasy about France and Spain having the power to block American trade access. Jefferson also decided to allow slavery in the acquired territory, which laid the foundation for the crisis of the Union a half century later. On the other hand, Napoleon Bonaparte was looking for ways to finance his empire's expansion, and he also had geopolitical motives for the deal. Upon completion of the agreement, Bonaparte stated, "This accession of territory affirms forever the power of the United States, and I have given England a maritime rival who sooner or later will humble her pride."

The purchase allowed Jefferson to plan something he had talked about since taking office: an expedition deep into the unmapped and largely unknown continent with the final destination being the Pacific Ocean. This could prove the most significant of the goals that Jefferson - a person who thought of himself as a scientifically-minded thinker - wanted to accomplish as president.[2]

The historical body of work on Jefferson's prior knowledge of the continent is well documented. Moreover, recent work demonstrates how "[b]y 1802, possibly after reading Mackenzie's recently published account of his Voyages from Montreal...through the Continent of North America, to the Frozen [Artic] and Pacific Oceans, Jefferson had begun to plan a serious voyage of discovery across the Mississippi to the Pacific."[3] He wanted, very much, for the U.S. to emulate previous voyages of scientific discovery. Something special lurked in his plans though. He possessed an ambitiousness that meant to not only learn about the continent, but launch an audacious journey that would leave the U.S. as the uncontested rulers of the continent. When scholarship confirms his mention of "'Mr. Lewis's tour,'" his crypticness shows this voyage "was to be like no other that he had contemplated and was to mounted on a scale unheard of before."[4] Doing so meant to produce a body of scientific knowledge that, more than anything else, would help the U.S. stake a claim to the entire continent. Science, then, could accomplish this. Herein, lay the true meaning of "Mr. Lewis's tour."

---

[2] " To the Western Ocean: Planning the Lewis and Clark Expedition." *Lewis and Clark: The Maps of Exploration 1507-1814* examines. http://www2.lib.virginia.edu/exhibits/lewis_clark/planning.html (accessed November 3, 2012).

[3] Konig, David Thomas. "Thomas Jeffersons Scientific Project and the American West." *Lewis and Clark: Journal to Another America, edited by Alan Taylor,* Missouri Historical Society Press (2003): 33

[4] Konig, David Thomas. "Thomas Jeffersons Scientific Project and the American West." *Lewis and Clark: Journal to Another America, edited by Alan Taylor,* Missouri Historical Society Press (2003): 33

Meriwether Lewis and William Clark

Against the advice of those who expected that France and Spain, colonial powers upon the continent, would object, Jefferson had already planned to send Lewis through the lands claimed by France and Spain. The historical body of scholarship is united in its appraisal of how, "[t]he political climate in 1803 complicated Jefferson's request." "He had asked Congress to authorize a military reconnaissance into unknown lands that already were claimed by the two most powerful nations in the world, France and Britain, with a third, Spain, clinging to a hold in the south and far west. Jefferson already had approached Spanish officials administering the region on behalf of France, seeking their approval to pass through the Louisiana Territory for the purposes of exploration. Spanish ambassador Don Carlos Martinez objected, but Jefferson pressed ahead with his request to Congress."[5]

With the Louisiana territory squarely in American possession, Jefferson could now embark upon his great plan. Cataloguing the diverse life within the region, as part of a voyage of scientific discovery, would in his estimation be on par with the great scientific journeys of the British. As some historians are quick to point out, "[t]empting as it is to see Lewis and Clark as unique - and as uniquely American - the larger sense the Corps of Discovery was one of a vast fleet of voyages that had set off since the early modern period to recover and bring home information about foreign places and foreign peoples."[6] The impulse to settle the U.S., dominate the continent, and have access to the oceans, for the purpose of trading with the "Orient," can be categorically defined as the same motivations of the European "Age of Discovery."

---

[5] "Circa 1803 (Living in America)." *Lewis and Clark: The Journey of the Corps of Discovery, A Film by Ken Burns.* http://www.pbs.org/lewisandclark/inside/idx_cir.html (accessed November 3, 2012).

[6] Valencius, Conevery Bolton. "Americans and Their Environments at the Time of Lewis and Clark." *Lewis and Clark: Journal to Another America, edited by Alan Taylor* Missouri Historical Society Press (2003): 150

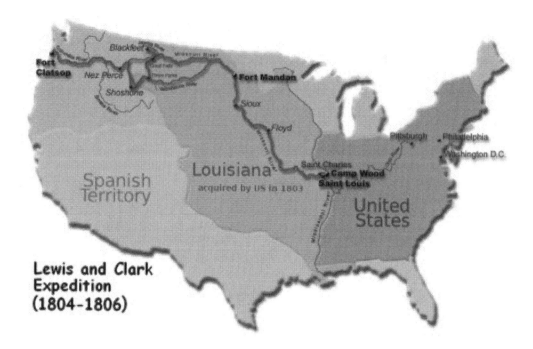

A map indicating the extent of the Louisiana Purchase

Jefferson was anxious about the American settlers on the frontier who might drift away from the Republic. Kingmakers and men of destiny could prove to be the worst thing the U.S. faced, and his own vice-president (Aaron Burr) would serve as the more stunning example. But of even greater concern was the quality of American settlements in the West. Jefferson wanted to spread American civilization and Republican institutions, not merely seed the wilderness with American stock. The way to approach the problem was to enrich the fortunes of the American settlers of this new vast territory. He had meant to do that by taking control of the Mississippi and New Orleans, knowing that their fortunes lay with access to trade and the ability to sell their products.

It is hard to determine exactly what Jefferson had in mind with Native Americans, other than his subscription to the idea of a "dying race to explain them." With this idea, one can see what Jefferson thought of their future, and perhaps what challenges, if any, they might present to an expanded Republic. However, he still had to deal with the present. "The West was not simply a blank slate during the early years of the Republic. The Indian peoples who inhabited the region constituted formidable obstacles to the progress of American settlement. But they also possessed invaluable information about the continent and its resources that Jefferson and his countrymen sought to exploit."[7]

Dealing with Native Americans in order to achieve national objectives proved pragmatic, in that the move merely followed the precedent established by other European powers by using commerce with indigenous nations as a pathway towards establishing commercial dominance in

---

[7] Onuf, Peter S. "Thomas Jefferson and the Expanding Union." *Lewis and Clark: Journal to Another America, edited by Alan Taylor* Missouri Historical Society Press (2003): 165

their colonies.[8] Jefferson was an imperialist who believed "American Indians were the guardians of 'soft gold' in every trade zone, jealously protecting the fur "capital" on their lands and harvesting a portion as 'interest' each season to purchase European manufacturers."[9] Jefferson meant to send Lewis and Clark to the west to negotiate superior terms as the new landlords. The tenants, in other words, could not charge interest; their profits required curtailment.

Dealing with the Natives was also in a sense a continuation of the American Revolution too, a struggle to spread Republican ideals in a political "wilderness," where the Natives required subjugation, lest the empire of liberty give way to alterNative societies of settlers, pale copies of their liberty-loving ancestors. "Jefferson conceived of conflicts along the frontier in ideological terms...War against the Indians - even a war that would lead to their removal or extermination - thus was seen as yet another phase of the Republican revolution against Old World tyranny and despotism."[10]

Jefferson also had to worry about the British, French, and Spanish, but not necessarily through armed conflict. The U.S merely needed to project "federal power into a contested region where European empires sought to establish influence and authority, and where Native peoples sought to secure their ancestral lands."[11] Natives could serve as potential allies in this great game of geopolitics, one that meant to "fundamentally alter the existing balance of power on the Northern Plains."[12] New flags would not be planted, but new proxies could be created to better serve the goals of the U.S. on the continent. Lewis and Clark would be the emissaries of this new "Great Father," and the "Indians" would be the "children."[13]

In what was perhaps America's most fabled journey, Lewis and Clark would find far more than they bargained for. The 33 men who made the trip came into contact with about two dozen Native American tribes, many of whom helped the men survive the journey, and along the way they met and were assisted by the famous Sacagawea, who would become one of the expedition's most famous participants. Though they suffered deaths on their way west, the group ultimately reached the Pacific coast and got back to St. Louis in 1806, having drawn up nearly 150 maps and giving America a good idea of much of what lay west.

---

[8] Fausz, J. Frederick. "Pacific Intentions: Lewis and Clark and the Western Fur Trade." *Lewis and Clark: Journal to Another America, edited by Alan Taylor,* Missouri Historical Society Press (2003): 120

[9] Fausz, J. Frederick. "Pacific Intentions: Lewis and Clark and the Western Fur Trade." *Lewis and Clark: Journal to Another America, edited by Alan Taylor,* Missouri Historical Society Press (2003): 122

[10] Onuf, Peter S. "Thomas Jefferson and the Expanding Union." *Lewis and Clark: Journal to Another America, edited by Alan Taylor* Missouri Historical Society Press (2003): 165

[11] Onuf, Peter S. "Thomas Jefferson and the Expanding Union." *Lewis and Clark: Journal to Another America, edited by Alan Taylor* Missouri Historical Society Press (2003): 175

[12] Cox, Wendel J. "A Journeys Beginning: The Corps of Discovery and the Diplomacy of Western Indian Affairs." *Lewis and Clark: Journal to Another America, edited by Alan Taylor* Missouri Historical Society Press (2003): 106, 114

[13] Fausz, J. Frederick. "Pacific Intentions: Lewis and Clark and the Western Fur Trade." *Lewis and Clark: Journal to Another America, edited by Alan Taylor,* Missouri Historical Society Press (2003): 133

Just through the diligent efforts of collecting samples and cataloguing their observations, the expedition made major contributions to the field of science, particularly in determining the geography of the place. Lewis and Clark did so with the production of dozens of maps that marked "their progress and meticulously recorded geographical detail as a guide to locating sites more precisely...The result revolutionized American notions of geography in general and of the West in particular." In essence, the continent became knowable and its accuracy served the interests of national ambitions. Making accurate maps accomplished just that, especially when "Clark made it clear that there existed no easy river-and-portage route to the Pacific." In this way, the failure to locate the fabled Northwest Passage did not end the dream of a route to the riches of the "Orient," but instead replaced them with a new map, where the new "orient" had been discovered in America's West. When "Clark recognized the presence of the American Indian and - significantly - recorded it on his maps," he created a new location for riches that American settlers could aspire towards in the great westward movements of the 19th century. While "it would take many more expeditions to disabuse Americans of such ideas," the maps produced by the expedition ensured future American settlers could become the masters of the continent. Accuracy served imperial ambitions, and "Lewis and Clark had made that possible."[14]

Jefferson had hoped commerce could be established by the efforts of the expedition through exploration and contact with natives, and both were established. The group discovered the best ways of passage through the terrain and established ways for future American settlers to travel from one distant point to another to trade. And of course, the expedition helped make contact with dozens of different tribes and descriptions of their similarities and differences. Lewis and Clark deserve recognition for accomplishing what Jefferson set out for them to do, "the critical first survey of distant Indian Country, and their greatest legacy was in publicizing and promoting the prospects for western profits among their fellow citizens."[15]

While America's historical memory of the expedition waned by the end of the century, the exploration made important contributions to the successive periods of expansion into the American West, contributions that can be qualified by the successes of American colonists and U.S. military conquest that came after the purchase of Louisiana. No one publicly claimed an "inheritance" won by Lewis and Clark, and there was no real proclamation of ownership over land, but there was a gradual expansion of control as white settlers pushed west. Westward movements displayed fitful starts and stops, and it would be another generation before Americans spoke about Manifest Destiny, but the expedition did validate earlier notions of perceived American hegemony over the continent. It just took events like the settlement of the

---

[14] Konig, David Thomas. "Thomas Jeffersons Scientific Project and the American West." *Lewis and Clark: Journal to Another America, edited by Alan Taylor,* Missouri Historical Society Press (2003): 42-43.
14

[15] Fausz, J. Frederick. "Pacific Intentions: Lewis and Clark and the Western Fur Trade." *Lewis and Clark: Journal to Another America, edited by Alan Taylor,* Missouri Historical Society Press (2003): 135.

"slavery issue," the biggest question of the nature of expansion, to decide how and where greater westward movements could begin. "Ultimately the establishment of American claims and enthusiasm for American settlement in this region required the new domestic and international contexts of the 1820, 1830s, and 1840s. In these new contexts, it was the mythic force of the expedition in American public consciousness, rather than its actual impact on American diplomatic claims, that proved most significant."[16]

Bridger's Early Years

James Felix Bridger was born on March 17, 1804, in Richmond, Virginia, on St. Patrick's Day. In terms of his later calling, the date is notable for being almost contemporaneous with the Lewis and Clark expedition by two years, which placed him squarely in the second and most comprehensive generation of Western exploration following the rudimentary beginnings of the Oregon Trail. As a result, Bridger would live to see the beginnings of modern development west of the Mississippi and the rise of cities such as Denver and Salt Lake City, much of it accomplished through his efforts.

Bridger's father, Patrick Henry Bridger, worked at every trade in which he could find an opening, from land surveyor and surgeon, to farmer and innkeeper. He married Chloe Tyler Bridger in the year before Bridger's birth, and operated an inn in Virginia. Bridger's sister, Virginia, was born in 1808. The construction of a rival hotel hampered business to the point where the family was forced to move in 1812.

At the age of 8, young Bridger found himself on a farm in the vicinity of St. Louis, Missouri, which was a small community at the time. For the remainder of his teen years, he worked in the rural setting of Six Mile Prairie, also known as the American Bottoms and DuPont Prairie, a short stretch of water away from St. Louis.

Partly through diverse interests, and partly through the geography of the area, Bridger learned many essential skills important to his eventual life path. He learned how to work with metal, pumping the bellows for blacksmith Phil Creamer; he learned how to handle a canoe, spending extensive hours every day on the river, exploring the locale. Since St. Louis could not be reached by any other way than water, Bridger became pilot for Antoine Dangen's passenger ferry. Despite his love for the river, he "disliked the average river man"[17] as he was both underemployed and overworked, unsteady in personal reliability, and prone to living as a vagabond. During these years, he also developed a comfort with weapons. It is said that by the time he struck out on his own, a gun at his side or in his hands was as "personal as a jacket."[18]

---

[16] Lewis, Jr, James E. "The Geopolitical Context of the Expedition." *Lewis and Clark: Journal to Another America, edited by Alan Taylor,* Missouri Historical Society Press (2003): 101.

[17] J. Cecil Alter, Jim Bridger, University of Oklahoma Press, 1925, 978-0-8061-1509-2

[18] J. Cecil Alter, Jim Bridger

Even though he was virtually illiterate and unable to sign his name, his diverse skills were immediately apparent, as was his "nearly photographic memory"[19] for terrain, including climate, bends in the river, and landmarks not noticeable to the average traveler.

The demands on each member of the Bridger family were such that a maiden aunt came to look after Bridger's younger sister, Virginia. St. Louis held many opportunities for Bridger's father, and the household slowly began to prosper, but personal losses incurred in the second decade of the century took away almost all of Bridger's family. The youngest sibling, born in 1812, died on the family farm in 1815. In the winter of that year, Bridger's mother was confined to the house and died in the summer of 1816. Patrick Bridger is said to have been beyond "heartbroken,"[20] and died himself in 1817.

At the age of 13, exploring the river with intermittent pay was no longer possible, as the young Bridger was forced to seek steady employment, but with a solid knowledge of machines, horses, guns, and river navigation, Bridger was prepared to enter the age of the mountain man, which most historians set as commencing around 1820 and lasting for at least the next two decades. Bridger joined his first trapping expedition in 1822, a trek up the Missouri River under William H. Ashley, and his close friend and partner, Andrew Henry. Ashley's experience in Missouri included bringing supplies to major settlements from New York by pack horse and steamship. He attained the rank of Brigadier General in the Missouri Territorial Militia in the year preceding the expedition, and his recruiting for young and skilled explorers included a call for "enterprising young men"[21] that instantly captivated Bridger, who, at 17, was to become the youngest member. Everywhere he turned, the advertisement tantalized him, appearing first in the *Missouri Gazette and Public Advertiser* on February 13, 1822 before being run in the *St. Louis Intelligencer* and various other papers throughout the region. Among his colleagues on the journey were several who would go on to make a name for themselves while working and surviving in the western mountains, including Hugh Glass, Jedediah Smith, William Sublette, and Jim Beckwourth.

---

[19] Yellowstone Genealogy Forum, James Felix Bridger, Yellowstone County, Feb. 18, 2004 – www.rootsweb.com/~mtygf/country/bridger-summary-htm

[20] Yellowstone Genealogy Forum

[21] Matthew Despain, Fred R. Gowans, James Bridger, Utah History to Go, Utah History Encyclopedia – www.historytogo.utah.gov/people/jamesbridger.html

Ashley

A depiction of Hugh Glass

Jedediah Smith

Early Expeditions

Bridger could not have signed on to a more enlightening project in terms of the dangers awaiting him west of the Mississippi. A month behind Ashley was a keelboat sent from St. Louis, carrying $10,000 worth of essential supplies. Barely 300 miles upriver from the departure point, the boat's mast was caught in an overhanging tree, turning it sideways and capsizing it moments later. Ashley was forced to arrange for a new boat and restock it. He returned from far up the river to personally escort the second boat in 1823.

The second attempt took the expedition farther upriver, into a region populated by the Arikara Indians, a tribe that took a particularly dim view of white strangers. Relations were never friendly, but disaster occurred after what had been termed a "nighttime violation"[22] of an Indian woman, which brought instant retribution. One of Ashley's men was killed in the altercation, and the entire Arikara tribe was roused against the trappers. On May 30, 70 of Ashley men were confronted by a force of Arikara numbering about 600. They attacked the trappers with London fuzils, a type of musket with exceptional accuracy with which the Arikara were considered to be "expert."[23] A call was sent out for military assistance, and Henry Leavenworth started up the Missouri River with a force of 200 regulars to rescue Ashley. He gathered 1,100 men along the way, including 700 Sioux. Nevertheless, in the first attack before Leavenworth's arrival, 15 of the Ashley party were killed when the well-armed Arikara opened fire.

Leavenworth

Soon after, Bridger found himself enlisted in a band of trappers turned guerilla fighters, as Andrew Henry led Ashley's men down the river to attack the Arikara villages "plaguing the mountains"[24] and interfering with trapping. In a joint effort with the newly-arrived reinforcements, Ashley and Leavenworth intended to make an example of the Arikara presence in the region. Despite the destruction of one village, Leavenworth never pressed the advantage of numerical superiority, and he eventually departed with the threat still present. In time, the region

---

[22] Mountain Men and Life in the Rocky Mountain West, Malachite's Big Hole, William Ashley – www.mman.us/ashley.htm
[23] History.com, 1823, Ashley's Trappers Attacked by Indians – www.history.com/this-day-in-history/ahsleys-trappers-attacked-by-indians
[24] Big Sky Words.com – Montana's Mountain Men: Jim Bridger – www.bigskywords.com/montana-blog/mountains-mountain-men-jim-bridger

was abandoned by the trapping trade. Even farther upriver, Ashley met with the same hostility from the vastly larger Blackfoot tribe, and was eventually forced to withdraw downriver. Bridger, however, went on to Yellowstone with Henry.

Having survived the various misfortunes suffered as one of "Ashley's Hundred,"[25] Bridger was connected to an infamous encounter along the trail, the accounts of which are still debated. Hugh Glass, entering a brushy area to check his traps, came across a pair of grizzly bear cubs, the mother a short distance away. His rifle rendered useless, Glass is said to have defended himself with a hunting knife, and was found by Bridger and Fitzpatrick, lying atop the dead bear, gravely injured. Other accounts from the few witnesses claim that the bear had been shot, although likely too late for saving Glass. Bridger and Glass had bonded at an attack on the Arikaras, assuming Bridger is the boy referred to in the historical accounts as "Jamie."[26] Glass rescued the young man during an Arikara raid. They spent much of that summer building the stockade and lodges for Fort Union at the confluence of the Missouri and Yellowstone rivers. For this reason, perhaps, Bridger agreed to stay with Glass, accompanied by Thomas Fitzpatrick, until his death, after which he would rejoin the company. The two reported back claiming that Glass had, indeed, died. Further inquiry raised the possibility the two had left Glass, alive and under threat of an Arikara attack, though no evidence was ever found of an Arikara presence in the area.

---

[25] Jeff Arnold's West, Jim Bridger in Fact and Fiction – www.jeffarnoldblogspot.com/2013/05/jim-bridger-in-fact-and-fiction.html
[26] Savages and Scoundrels, Jim Bridger – www.savagesandscoundrels.org/people/savages-scoundrels/jim-bridger/

A contemporary depiction of Glass being mauled

Glass, meanwhile, awoke in a shallow grave filled with loose dirt and covered with leaves. He had no weapons, a broken leg, and cuts so deep his back ribs were exposed. He reset his own leg, allowed the maggots to devour the dead flesh, and literally crawled a distance of 100 miles to the Cheyenne River. There, he fashioned a crude raft and floated downriver. Wrapped in the hide of the attacking bear, he made his way another hundred miles to Ft. Kiowa with an advanced infection and high fever.

After a painfully slow recovery, Glass pursued both Bridger and Fitzpatrick with revenge on his mind. Bridger's constant movement around the West was in part spurred by the "recurring theme"[27] of Glass's pursuit. He evaded a confrontation for years, but once caught, he was forgiven for committing "a youthful transgression."[28] Glass withheld his wrath from Fitzpatrick as well when he discovered that his second betrayer had joined the army, and was stationed at Ft. Atkinson, Wisconsin. The details of the account were open to serious question, but no witnesses could testify as to which components of the tale were true.

Biographer J. Cecil Alter, a retired weather bureau official, took it upon himself to attempt a

---

[27] Bozeman Daily Chronicle, Ben Pierce, Outdoor Editor, Jim Bridger : The Man, The Myth, The Legend, January 28, 2016
[28] BigSkywords.com

definitive biography of Bridger in the first half of the 20th century. According to several critics, his effort was "the best biography to date."[29] Alter, however, took grave exception to any part of the story suggesting Bridger would abandon a friend in such a woeful condition. In dismissing popular accounts, he observes that for Bridger to be "party to such a lapse from heroic conduct"[30] would run against every other testament to his life. He further claims that if the account of his abandonment of Glass is taken out of the historical record, it "removes the only serious blemish"[31] from the great explorer's reputation.

The contract Bridger signed with the Ashley expedition required all members to remain in the general's employ for at least one year, and a maximum of three. The original group spent many months in one another's company. For Bridger, it was a learning experience from older explorers, and the forming of lifelong friendships should he possess the good fortune to survive the hostile West. At the onset of Ashley expeditions deep into the interior, a trapper stood an approximate 50/50 chance of survival within the first year.

Indeed, a good share of Bridger's friends met with violent deaths. Among his most colorful colleagues was Jedediah Smith, famous for his Bible-reading around the campfire. He once fancied that the young Bridger looked very much like the Angel Gabriel, and dubbed him "Old Gabe," one of many nicknames to come. Able to go months or years without any social contact among the settler population, the mountain men were highly social with each other. Jim Beckwourth was the only African-American trapper in the Ashley expedition. As good a yarn-spinner as Bridger, he is among the only trappers who took the trouble to record their life stories. Early historians are unkind to Beckwourth, one of them going so far as to call him a "gaudy liar."[32] Later sources describe the first historians of the mountain man culture as refusing give credence to a "mongrel with mixed blood."[33]

Either way, the culture of being alone threw off almost all conventions of social propriety, including dress and personal hygiene. In general, the mountain man "took the weather as it came,"[34] generally declining to sleep in tents or structures other than an occasional makeshift shelter. The mountain man worldview held that one was safer from sickness sleeping under the stars than in an enclosure. Most members of the fraternity carried only one set of clothes, and those with more did not change for months at a time, even at the loners' annual, legendary, rendezvous meetings.

---

[29] J. Cecil Alter, Rugged Mountain Man, Review by Wayne Gard, Southwest Review Vol. 48 No. 3, Summer Fiction Special (Summer 1963) p. 305, Southern Methodist University

[30] J. Cecil Alter, Wayne Gard

[31] J. Cecil Alter, Wayne Gard

[32] Beckwourth.org, James Pierson Beckwourth, 1798-1866, Museum of the Mountain Man – www.museumofthemountainman.com/product/jim-beckwourth/

[33] Beckwourth.org

[34] Stanley Vestal, Jim Bridger, Mountain Man: A Biography, Bookrags – www.bookrags.com/studyguide-jim-bridger-mountain-man/quotes.html#gsc,tab=0

The rendezvous celebrations were held in locales throughout the West, and some rode, hiked, or rafted many miles to attend. The idea of a rendezvous was not merely a loose-knit agreement among trappers to visit one another at an unspecified time, but a system of events that could be likened to a modern trade fair. The concept of a rendezvous was put into practice by General Ashley, who had "introduced the rendezvous system as a substitute for traditional trading posts."[35] A social occasion for storytelling and drinking, it was also the only way to hear the news of the world before reentering the wilderness. Since the mountain men were trappers, and since beaver was their prime prey, the air was rife with the odor of castoreum, "an odiferous oily secretion of the beaver."[36] In contrast to the gold of fresh-tanned hides prized by fur hat designers and merchants in the fashion industry to the east, this substance was summed up by one historian in no uncertain terms as "Black. Dirty Black, greasy Black, shiny Black, bloody Black, stinky Black. Black."[37] Naturally, clean silverware was not in use in Western country, and mountain men wiped their knives and forks, when available, on their clothes when eating, and directly after skinning animals, including the beaver.

Scarcely back from the Ashley expedition, Bridger turned around and went farther upriver again, into the Yellowstone with Henry, traveling up to 1,000 miles mostly on keelboats, approximating much of the original Lewis and Clark route. In the following years, he trapped without pause along known Western routes with various companies and in diverse partnerships. In 1823 and 1824, he trapped as a member of John Weber's party, wintering in the Bighorn region in Montana and Wyoming country. Born near Hamburg, Weber had come to the United States in 1807, and was a member of Ashley's first expedition leading one of the "trapping brigades,"[38] when the party split at the mouth of the Yellowstone. In 1825, he attended the Cache Valley Rendezvous on Cub Creek near what is now Cove, Utah. Bridger was also present, and witnessed a great speculative debate on the true course of the Bear River.

Under Weber's employ at the time, Bridger was selected to travel the length of the river's course and report back in detail. After an extensive journey, Bridger reported that, in his opinion, he had discovered an arm of the Pacific Ocean in Utah country, due to the saltiness of the water. In hindsight, he had clearly reached the "vast lake,"[39] later named the Great Salt Lake, by the shores of which Salt Lake City would soon be established. Some accounts claim Bridger to be the first white man to see the lake, while others give the honor to Étienne Provost, a similarly skilled mountain man from Quebec. Much of the region later took parts of Provost's name for the names of towns, such as Provo. During expeditions with Weber, Bridger also became one of the first Europeans to see Yellowstone's geysers.

---

[35] Encyclopaedia Britannica, William Henry Ashley – www.britannica.com/biography/William-Henry-Ahsley
[36] Wyoming Tales and Trails, Rendezvous – www.wyomingtalesandtrails.com/fur2.html
[37] Wyoming Tales and Trails, Rendezvous
[38] Utah Division of State History, John Weber – www.heritage.utah.gov/uhg-people-weber-john
[39] XRoads, James Bridger, 1804, University of Virginia – www.xroads.virginia.edu/-hyper/hns/mtmen/jimbridger.html

Provost

Old Faithful at Yellowstone

By 1825, Bridger was once again working for General Ashley and the Rocky Mountain Fur Company. Ultimately, Bridger returned from the Green River Rendezvous with Ashley's party and reached the Bighorn River collectively carrying $50,000 worth of fur packs–over a million dollars by modern standards. To risk losing such a bonanza due to an error while rafting the river was unthinkable, and all but Bridger took the Bad Pass Trail. On a small raft built from driftwood, Bridger attempted the feat of riding the river, not really knowing what lay ahead. Despite numerous passages through daunting rapids, he emerged from the canyon unscathed, to the amazement of the party. The feat is the first recorded float of its kind. His account was published more than three decades later, but is still relatively unknown among his achievements in Western exploration.

In the winter of 1826, Bridger attended the second Cache Valley Rendezvous, after a season under constant attack by the Blackfoot tribe. Among the various meetings around the region, the 1826 Cache Valley Rendezvous was a particular "highlight of the trapper's year."[40] He made a handsome profit from trapping that year, and developed friendships among fellow explorers, not to mention a loyal following that would serve him well as he took over expeditions. When Ashley left the fur trade, Bridger was among those who bought out his share of the Rocky Mountain Fur Co., which continued to operate successfully through the rest of the decade.

For the moment, however, storytelling was the best part of the rendezvous, near what is now Laketown, Utah. Bridger was said to be without equal in this fireside art, and in one example, he cast a spell over a group of Sioux and Cheyenne for over an hour, using only sign language to weave his unlikely tales. One of Bridger's most notable biographers, Grenville Dodge, described his nature as "companionable…tall…straight as an arrow,"[41] with a slim but powerful physique, and an abundant head of hair, even in his old age. Surprisingly, for one so fond of traveling alone, he was reportedly an amiable, agreeable person, "hospitable and generous…[with] a mild expression."[42] With his masterful storytelling, he "loved to shock"[43] groups of easterners, Europeans, and "tenderfeet"[44] in their first visits to the American interior. Eager to convince his guests one absurdity after another were true, he described a range of mountains made of pure glass, towering above the forests to the west. A captivated audience leaned even further in when he told them the mountain stood between him and an elk. Missing shot after shot, Bridger told them, he finally realized the mountain was like a magnifying glass, and that the animal was really 20 miles away. He maintained, with a straight face, that Pike's Peak began as a deep hole in the ground. He regaled the uninitiated with stories of petrified forests in which petrified birds sang to him as he passed by, With the Yellowstone geysers clearly in mind, he spoke of a lake with a hot surface, but cool in the depths. Within his favorite fishing holes, he would often catch fish and have them cooked as they were brought to the surface. It is no surprise that when Bridger told stories of having seen the Yellowstone geysers as they really were, no one believed him, so dubious were his other stories. In his words, "They said I was the damnedest liar ever lived."[45] Among his audience's favorites was the surprise ending to a tale in which a group of Cheyenne chased him into a box canyon where he became trapped. When an eager listener asked what happened next, Bridger paused before replying, "Well, they killed me."[46] His abiding advice for anyone entering Indian country was far more valuable fireside fare: "Where there ain't no Indians, you'll find 'em the thickest."[47] For those who were less amused by his ravings, he responded that it was improper for him to have "spoilt a good story just for the sake of the truth."[48]

---

[40] Xroads, Jim Bridger
[41] Xroads, Jim Bridger
[42] Xroads, Jim Bridger
[43] Xroads, Jim Bridger
[44] Xroads, Jim Bridger
[45] John A. Hogwood, Review of Jim Bridger by J. Cecil Alter, *California Historical Social Quarterly*, Vol. 43 No. 3 (September 1964) p. 257
[46] Frederick J. Chiaventone, Jim Bridger, Cowboys & Indians Magazine – www.cowboysandindians.com/2015/05/jim-bridger/
[47] John A. Hogwood

With respect to the 1827 and 1828 meetings held in Cache Valley near Bear Lake on Utah's border with Wyoming, it is likely Bridger attended both events, as well as the Ogden-Gardner Rendezvous near the present community of Mount Green.

Biographer Norman B. Wiltsey dubbed Bridger the odd name of "He-Coon,"[49] his 19th century term for a storyteller of the first order, in the vernacular of the mountain men. Wiltsey pays tribute to the vast expanses Bridger undertook and the breadth of his experience saying, "Wherever his stick floated–there Jim went."[50] On a sadder note, the author suggests Bridger knew the Native American in a deeper way than any other white man. Attuned to changes in the ways of men and nature in his forest paradise, Bridger understood, before anyone else, that the "ancient hunter's"[51] way of life could not survive European civilization's advance across the continent.

Pushing West

By 1830, that instinct had borne out. Intense competition for the fur trade in the West arrived in the form of John Jacob Astor's American Fur Co., forcing trappers for the Rocky Mountain Fur Company into increasingly hostile areas of Blackfoot country. The situation worsened with the arrival of the Hudson Bay Company that had all but dominated East Coast trapping in previous decades. By that year, Bridger was one of five full partners in the Rocky Mountain Company, and under considerable duress to continue the success of previous years, but he was also comfortable commanding the expeditions as an "able"[52] brigade leader, somehow avoiding Indian attacks year after year and still managing to turn a profit. His thoughts did, however, turn to other forms of employment, as his knowledge of Western terrain was prized by settlers, religious movements, and the U.S. government as danger mounted.

In 1832, his luck ran out when he was finally caught in hostile action with the Blackfoot tribe. Able to escape, he nevertheless carried two arrows in his back, one of them for a period of three years after the point broke off deep within his flesh. Relief came when he met Dr. Marcus and Narcissa Whitman on their way to establish a mission in the Walla Walla Valley. A medical doctor as well, Whitman removed the arrowhead without the benefit of anesthesia. As several Indians, including Blackfeet, looked on, Bridger bore up well under the surgery that dislodged the arrowhead from underneath a bone and surrounded by cartilage. One Indian observed that he had a big heart, like a Blackfoot, and Bridger did not seem to appreciate the remark.

That year marked a tragedy for rendezvous participants in the Pacific Northwest, as well. Bridger and all his notable comrades were present at the Pierre Hole Rendezvous, held up the

---

[48] Frederick J. Chiaventone
[49] Norman B. Wiltsey, He-Coon of the Mountain Men, Montana: the Magazine of Western History, Vol. 6 No. 1 (Winter 1956) p. 11
[50] Norman B. Wiltsey
[51] Norman B. Wiltsey
[52] Xroads, Jim Bridger

Snake River. To put the Pierre Hole event in perspective, the Nez Perce erected 120 lodges, while the Flatheads, who had come from Montana country, had over 80. Dripps and Fontenelle were represented by 90 trappers, and the Rocky Mountain Fur Company sent 100. Sublette and Campbell brought another 100, along with "assorted independents"[53] and a caravan from John Jacob Astor's American Fur Company.

When the rendezvous ended, groups of trappers headed off in various directions. William Sublette's party traveled seven miles up the Snake River where they met a large party of Gros Ventre Indians, translated as "big belly."[54] Antoine Godin and his sidekick, a Flathead named Baptiste Dorian, went forward to greet the chief. When someone yelled at Dorian to shoot, he killed the chief at close range and stole his coveted red blanket before retreating into the main group of trappers. A battle immediately ensued, and joined by larger groups of trappers, eventually grew to a force of 200. The incident raged throughout the day, and by nightfall, 20 Indians and 26 trappers lay dead.

In his capacity as guide for private expeditions, Bridger ran across more than one wealthy eccentric, most of who were upper-class malcontents from Europe, Britain in particular. By the end of 1832, he led Scottish adventurer Captain Sir William Drummond Stewart on a hunting expedition, and to the Ham's Creek Rendezvous. As the second brother in his family, Stewart did not enjoy the same benefits as his elder sibling. Following a violent row between them, Stewart made good on his intent to escape British society and traveled to New York to seek an American-style adventure. From there, he received an introduction to William Clark and moved on to St. Louis, taking artist Alfred Jacob Miller along with him to chronicle his journeys in paintings and sketches. Further introductions were made to Chouteau, Ashley, and Bridger, and before long, he was off on an authentic Western hunt, complete with white shooting pants and his trademark Panama hat.

---

[53] Legends of America, Jim Bridger, Quintessential Guide of the Rocky Mountains – www.legendsofamerica.com/we-jimbridger.html
[54] Legends of America, Jim Bridger

A portrait of Stewart

Though his finances back home began to wither, he was, for a time, regarded as a "wilderness prince."[55] In every way, Stewart "fell in love with the people, scenery, and life."[56] Rather than behaving as the arrogant, foreign snob as expected, he pitched in, learning everything he could about trapper life and the indigenous peoples of every region he visited. Not merely a paying guest - like his fellow traveler John Harrison, the son of President William Henry Harrison and father of president-to-be Benjamin Harrison - he "accepted every duty that came his way,"[57] no matter how mundane, dangerous, or unpleasant. In a short time, he was given important responsibilities, and fulfilled his duties admirably. Stewart felt little draw toward his European home, and stayed in the wilderness for a full seven years. When, at last, he did return to Scotland, he luxuriated in the Miller sketches adorning the walls of Murthly Castle. His remaining years were spent entertaining and feuding with the surviving members of his family.

---

[55] Mountain Men and Life in the Rocky Mountain West, Sir William Drummond Stewart – www.mman.us/stewartwilliamdrummond.htm
[56] Mountain Men and Life in the Rocky Mountain West
[57] Mountain Men and Life in the Rocky Mountain West

John Harrison

Meanwhile, over the following years, Bridger opened travel routes through new country between Utah, Wyoming, and Montana, including the Sylvan Trail in East Yellowstone, to the Grand Canyon. Sylvan was a mountain pass of moderate elevation through the Absaroka Range, the only possibility for entering Yellowstone from the east. He found himself fascinated with the Firehole River in northwest Wyoming, which flows through a geyser basin including the well-known Old Faithful. He was equally taken with the Obsidian Cliffs of Yellowstone, standing at 7,400 feet above sea level and boasting half a mile of black volcanic glass from which ancient people forged their tools.

The Rocky Mountain Fur Company was officially dissolved in 1834, but Bridger continued to traverse enormous sections of the West, trapping or being employed as a guide. In 1835, he married Cora Insala, the first of his three Native American wives, at the urging of her father, a Flathead chief. Historical evidence exists to suggest the two had already known each other, but as one observer put it, she was "the prettiest thing 'Jim' had ever seen."[58] Bridger married her almost immediately and the two traveled together extensively. Throughout this marriage, he took on the nickname of Blanket Chief due to the blanket she made for him. Mary Ann Bridger, their first daughter, was born in 1836. Three years later, Cora and Mary Ann were taken back to Missouri for safekeeping and schooling with family.

---

[58] Ted Stillwell: Jim Bridger, Blanket Chief, The Examiner – www.examiner.net/news/20160817/ted-stillwell-jim-bridger-blanket-chief

Returning to the trail, Bridger went through St. Louis to see his younger sister, Virginia, and as always, headed immediately toward the West. By the end of the year, he had returned to Idaho country from Yellowstone, where his relationship with the regional tribes was far more temperate than it had been in earlier encounters in Wyoming and Montana. Among the native people of the northwest, Bridger was known as Big Throat, after the large goiter that continued to grow on his neck. Speculation at the time suggested he had drunk too much spring water. Through 1837, he worked with Kit Carson, the legendary trapper and soldier, at Yellowstone. He also worked with Joe Meek, a fellow trapper six years his junior, who ended up in Oregon Territory as a sheriff and U.S. Marshall. Both men lost a daughter as a result of the Whitman Mission massacre in Walla Walla.

Carson

The seemingly inexhaustible supply of beaver pelts in the West began to dry up by 1840, and many leading trappers returned to civilization. Even Bridger was said to have grown weary of his nomadic life. Numbers crossing the established Oregon Trail swelled as missionaries and emigrant settlers braved the journey from Missouri. Bridger, now with a wife and two children, was perfectly suited to offer services to such travelers, ranging from provisions to expedition leadership and chart-making. No area of frontier life was unfamiliar to him, and despite the lack of formal education, he was able to communicate fluently with virtually any culture to cross his path. His linguistic skills included French, Spanish, and six Native American dialects, and various tribes often requested his mediating skills for local disputes with settlers. He dealt with local Indian populations in conjunction with what remained of the beaver trade without having to trek hundreds of miles.

By the summer of 1840, Bridger and his trapping partner, Pierre Louis Vasquez, had planned and constructed a group of buildings on the west bank of the Green River of Utah. Besides its use as a trapping base, there was a small store and blacksmith shop for "a supply of iron on the Road of the Emigrants on Black's Fork of Green River."[59] Six years Bridger's elder, Vasquez had also answered General Ashley's advertisement in Missouri for the first trapping expedition. He went on to become the most famous early trapper in Colorado, personally building Fort Convenience and a hunter's cabin in the region. He also built Fort Vasquez on the South Platte River. Vasquez would stay with the post for another 15 years before retiring to Bridger's home town of Westport, Missouri.

The waystation was completed just in time for the first wagons to pass through, and it served as the first such post for trading with emigrants for things other than furs. The stop came to be known as Fort Bridger, long before it would come into use for that purpose. Located in what is now Uinta County, Wyoming, Fort Bridger served as a hub for those traveling the Oregon Trail, the California Trail, or the Mormon Trail into the Salt Lake basin. The original "fort" featured two double log houses approximately 40 feet in length, joined in the center by a horse pen. In terms of access to established landmarks, it lay 478 miles northwest of Denver, and 124 miles northeast of Salt Lake. The fort sat at an elevation of 7,000 feet, and was situated in the center of a green pasture. Two large swinging gates stood at the entrance, large enough for a team of cattle to pass through, and sturdy enough to protect against an attack.

By this time, Bridger was known as "Colonel Bridger," and was considered a "shrewd"[60] trader. In fact, during these years, contact with the emigrating public brought out a previously unknown impoliteness in the solitary trapper. He was increasingly fond of tobacco, appeared "uncouth in dress,"[61] and had taken to drinking "for his stomach's sake."[62] Despite the scarcity of beavers in the West by the early 1840s due to the over-trapping by the three major fur companies, other wildlife abounded, and Bridger readily offered his services as a guide to eastern and foreign guests who craved the thrill of killing big-game in the new country. Among the most eccentric of his clients was Sir George Gore of England, a notorious big-game hunter who had already sought adventure throughout Africa and Asia. To the simple Westerners' astonishment, Gore arrived for his expedition with a fleet of more than 50 servants and a supply cache that included a shiny, brass bedstead and marble washstand. Among his hunting weaponry was a British bayonet, and an array of British-style stalker-hats. Among his servants was a personal valet and one gentleman, engaged only to tie flies to the line on fishing expeditions. Gore's list went on to include "112 horses, 12 yoke of oxen, 14 dogs, six wagons, and 21 carts. He was accompanied by 40 armed game executioners, all carrying heavy sporting rifles."[63] On one occasion, Gore presented Bridger with the gift of an entire suit of English armor, and the wily trapper took no small delight in wearing it in camp and clanking around, much to the shock of

---

[59] Xroads, Jim Bridger
[60] Overland.com, Jim Bridger – www.overland.com/jimbridger.html
[61] Overland.com
[62] Overland.com
[63] Norman B. Wiltsey

his Indian friends. In a display of horrific damage to the natural environment, Gore and his hired mob shot 40 grizzly bears and 2,500 buffalo, deer, elk, and antelope on his various trips. In that era, white visitors from the East had not yet considered the possibility that Western resources might be finite. Bridger paid special attention to Gore, in part because he read to his guide every night around the campfire. On hearing the works of Shakespeare for the first time, Bridger observed that he'd never heard the language spoken so beautifully. Years later, he would recite entire speeches from only one hearing. He also reportedly showed a particular fascination with the tales of Napoleon and Waterloo.

As for the hunting, Bridger was shocked at Gore's appetite. The adventurer seemed to want a specimen of everything that either ran, swam, or flew in the American West. In Bridger's words, "I got plumb sick o' killin…[I] ain't seen so much blood and guts at one time."[64] As for Gore, once he had tired of the West, the remainder of Bridger's time as a guide was spent with various army units in possession of poorly developed charts and little firsthand experience when it came to new trails being forged in the west.

Bridger used a portion of the handsome wages paid by Gore to visit Washington, D.C. in order to plead his case before President Buchanan against the Mormons' destruction of his property. By all accounts, he was initially given the typical Washington, D.C. run-around, but he eventually got through to the president. He was not to receive compensation for his loss, but once ready to return to the West, federal troops followed under his guidance. A showdown with the Mormon leadership seemed inevitable.

In the business of advising settlers, Bridger was now privy to the Hastings Cutoff, sold to the emigrating population as a more favorable route to California in lieu of Oregon. However, the route was newly discovered and not thoroughly explored or charted, and many considered it an "unproven risk."[65] Despite the shorter distance by 61 miles, the dangers of the California route were aptly demonstrated by the story of the Donner Party, a large number of which perished on the southern route. Some lay part of the blame at Bridger's feet for not making more of an effort to dissuade them, but the nature of those conversations cannot be precisely known. Wagons had used the route before the months preceding the Donner Party, but July 31 was too late in the year for an attempt to travel what is now Interstate 80. All seemed well until a note was found, warning them to stay away from the Weber Canyon route. They complied but lost even more crucial time. Struggling into Nevada at last, the party became snowbound, and nearly half of it perished, with some survivors resorting to cannibalism.

Cora Insala Bridger, daughter of Little Chief, or Scarface of the Flatheads, died at Fort Bridger in 1845 during the birth of the couple's third child. In the same year, Bridger married again, this time a Colorado Ute named Two Fawns. Their son, born soon thereafter, was named Rocky

---

[64] Norman B. Wiltsey
[65] Utah State History

Mountain Felix. Still, new home life did little to restrain Bridger from extensive exploration, particularly with the influx of Mormons arriving from the east in search of a route into the American southwest. When Brigham Young was searching for a permanent home for members of the Church, he met with Bridger to discuss the Salt Lake region. Although Bridger was generally opposed to Mormon settlements in Utah and dubious as to the likelihood of the Church thriving there, the conversations were at first amiable. At Young's insistence, Bridger eventually drew him a map on the ground with a stick, all the while warning against the difficulties of agriculture in such a place. He had realized the Mormon presence had "sapped"[66] a good portion of his trade away, creating instant economic trouble for the post.

Young

---

[66] United States History, Jim Bridger

The map, as it turned out, had been drawn with uncanny accuracy, a fact not lost on other emigrant expeditions and the military. In hindsight, Captain John Gunnison, with whom Bridger had worked more than once, reported to his superiors that "with a buffalo skin and a piece of charcoal, [Bridger] will map out any portion of this vast region with wonderful accuracy."[67] Colonel Collins, who explored the South Pass around the west side of the Windy Mountains with Bridger, concurred, noting, "As a guide, he was without equal. [He] could smell his way when he could not see it."[68] Brigham Young agreed, as his flock had found their Salt Lake home by way of the path Bridger had etched in the dirt, which was an alternate route through an openly hostile terrain and climate.

The sheer force of the Mormon population soon became a moral force in the region, and Bridger was on the wrong side of the Mormon view when it came to almost everything. This led to vehement arguments between Young and Bridger about selling alcohol and guns to the Indians and his handing out printed misinformation about the Church in an attempt to turn the indigenous tribes against it. The truth of these accusations is in question, at least on the scale imagined by Young. At first, the Church leader lacked the political clout with which to uproot Bridger, but in 1847, the bulk of Mormon settlers arrived. Once organized, the numbers established the Church's dominance over the region, wielding political, economic, and moral power over the previously sparse population. Young was appointed Territorial Governor of Utah country by President Millard Fillmore, a position in which he "served fervently."[69] In this role, he was personally responsible for the immigration of 16.000 Mormons to the territory and convinced 80,000 converts to migrate from Britain, Western Europe, and Scandinavia. He was personally involved in the development of 350 settlements, as well. In the face of all this, Bridger found himself at a decided disadvantage.

Also in 1847, the family and wards of Marcus Whitman were massacred by members of the Cayuse in Walla Walla, believing Dr. Whitman to have intentionally poisoned their people. A measles epidemic of European origin had cut a swath through the Indian nations in the northwest, and when the Chief's son died, retribution was certain. Bridger's daughter, Mary Ann, was in the kitchen recovering from the measles herself when she was abducted. She later died from her injuries. Narcissa Whitman had been her personal caretaker and had been with the Whitman family for well over a year. The local announcement printed soon after read, "Mary Ann Bridger, aged 13, died at the residence of A.L. Hedges in this city."[70] A brief article went on to describe the young girl as being 11 years of age and the "half-Indian daughter of Jim Bridger."[71] Citing that she had left the mission to attend the Whitman Mission School, she was not spared from danger as the school sat on Mission land close to the house. The *Oregon*

---

[67] WyoHistory.org, A Map of the West in His Head: Jim Bridger, Guide to Plains and Mountains – www.wyohistory.org/encyclopedia/jim-bridger
[68] WyoHistory.org
[69] Legends of America
[70] Oregon Spectator, March 23, 1848, p.3.6
[71] Oregon Spectator

Spectator added that she possessed "a mild disposition."[72]

Bridger's second wife died in 1849 of complications from childbirth, a common tragedy in that era, but once again, he was not to be alone for long. In 1850, Chief Washakie of the Shoshones offered his daughter to Bridger, who married for a third time. Calling her by the name of Mary, the two spent their summers at Fort Bridger but wintered with the Shoshones. She is often cited as belonging to a Shoshone subset of the Snake Indians.

Conflicts

Bridger spent most of 1850 as a guide for Major Howard Stansbury, under orders from the U.S. Army Corps of Topographical Engineers to chart the Salt Lake region. Mormon passions were roused by the expedition, which the Church viewed as an attempt by the U.S. government to expel them from the territory, or worse. Stansbury met with Brigham Young to reassure him that this was not the case. Requiring a shorter route than the South Pass of the Oregon Trail, Stansbury sought Bridger out to devise a shorter route. He guided Stansbury through a pass south of the Great Basin, later known as Bridger's Pass. This new route was later employed by the overland mail system, the Union Pacific Railroad, and for the construction of Interstate 80. The expedition successfully reached Salt Lake, and in addition to charting the region, flora and fauna were catalogued, possible coal deposits were located, and railroad and telegraph development were facilitated. In the same year, Utah became an official territory, with Brigham Young continuing to serve as Territorial Governor.

The conflict between Bridger and Brigham Young soon turned to action once the Mormons controlled the political system of the territory. Young had a separate post built, which he named Fort Supply, in part to wrest Mormon business from Bridger, the profligate non-believer. In 1853, Young sent the Nauvoo Legion, a much-feared Mormon militia, after Bridger to arrest him and suspend his license to do business in the Territory. The Legion was established decades before as protection from Missouri's Mormon Extermination Order, and thrived in the Church's new home of Illinois. Revived in the Utah Territory, it spent much time subduing enclaves of hostile Indians intent on wiping out the new Mormon presence. Bridger received news of Young's directive in time and was able to flee, but the "guerilla militia force"[73] stormed Bridger's post, took it over, and burned it to the ground. Oddly, the Church's own Fort Supply was destroyed as well. When the U.S. Army arrived to settle the disturbance, they discovered a fighting force very nearly equal to their own. The Nauvoo Legion stampeded the army cattle and harassed the troops in every way possible, resulting in an opening for the Mormon Wars in the Utah Territory.

The church officially purchased the ruined buildings from Vasquez in 1853, paying Bridger's partner $8,000, half of the purchase price. Bridger was not to receive his portion of the sale for

---

[72] Oregon Spectator
[73] HistoryGlobe.com, The Oregon Trail – www.historyglobe.com/ot/fortbridger.htm

some time. Fort Supply was rejuvenated as a service to Mormon travelers dealing directly with the Church. It sat 12 miles southwest and between the two facilities in which the church had invested $60,000 in what they referred to as their "twin endeavors."[74]

Spending the year of 1856 well away from the growing Utah conflict, Bridger served as guide for the Lieutenant Warren Expedition around the Black Hills of modern South Dakota and the Yellowstone River. Warren was instructed to reconnoiter the region, and Bridger led the expedition from Fort Union to the mouth of the Yellowstone before heading northwest to the mouth of the Powder River. Bridger's party reached as far as what came to be known as Colter's Hell, a plethora of steaming rivers and hot springs around modern-day Cody, Wyoming. Since he was a famed story-teller, no one believed him until official military reports had been publicized. The Warren Expedition "revealed"[75] that a great deal of geographical information was still lacking to support future development. Warren recommended further exploration into regions still classified as "terra incognito,"[76] with Bridger as guide. He would return to the Montana and Wyoming regions to lead other expeditions over the next several years.

Brigham Young's conflict with Bridger was only one of several reasons President James Buchanan ultimately sent U.S. Army troops into the Utah Territory. The action was a preparation for what became known as the Mormon Wars, beginning in 1857 and continuing through the following year. The larger reason for Buchanan's decision was a political one. At that time, slavery was still tied to the economy, making it a difficult target without serious recriminations. Polygamy, however, was ripe for action, as virtually no one accepted it as a practice, with the exception of the Latter Day Saints. Dissatisfied with the direction in which Young was taking the Territory, Buchanan replaced him with a new man named Alfred Cumming, but the President neglected to inform Young of the change.

---

[74] BigSkywords.com
[75] Discovering Lewis & Clark, Warren's Lower Yellowstone – www.lewis-clark.org/article/1151
[76] Discovering Lewis & Clark

Buchanan

Cumming

Colonel Albert Sidney Johnston, best known for being mortally wounded while leading the Confederate army at the Battle of Shiloh in April 1862, was assigned the task of escorting the new governor to Utah, and he hired Jim Bridger as the most qualified guide to ensure their safe arrival. Johnston led 2,500 men from Fort Leavenworth in the midst of winter and suffered greatly for it, losing many horses and mules, but had he not hired Bridger, the extent of the disaster could have been far worse.

Johnston

Bridger was given the rank of Major for what would become more an invasion of Salt Lake City than a diplomatic mission, considering that the Legion swore that it would burn it down. That Bridger would take an interest in guiding the U.S. government against the Mormons can be easily understood, since the Church had taken over his post and he had not yet been paid for it. The Nauvoo Legion attempted to harass the troops without causing bloodshed, but it could not always be avoided. In the Mountain Meadows Massacre, the Mormons, with elements of local tribes, attacked a wagon train heading for California, believing it was a convoy of army supply wagons. Young's "Corps of Observation"[77] continually spied on troop movements. Once Johnston had occupied Salt Lake City, hostilities eased, Cummings was allowed to take his post, and the Mormons received a general pardon.

It was rumored, although never proven, that Bridger had taken a fourth wife from the Mormons on July 4 of the following year, which would have set him squarely against Buchanan's anti-

---

[77] BigSkywords.com

polygamy campaign. Such a theory is suspect, to say the least. Of Bridger's famed colleagues in the Utah War, Johnston died at Shiloh, while Brigham Young's apprentice, William Frederick Cody, became the legendary Buffalo Bill. Bridger remained furious for the rest of his life that the incident had been forgiven, and that Brigham Young, of all people, had received a full pardon.

Bridger's return to the Yellowstone region came at the behest of the U.S. War Department. In 1859, he led an "exploring, mapping party"[78] from Fort Pierre in the Dakota Territory to Fort Laramie, the Bighorns, Bitterroot Valley, and on to Fort Benton. The budget for the exhaustive expedition came to $60,000, and Bridger was paid a handsome $125 per month. William F. Raynolds led a 30-man military detachment as protection for the work of eight technicians. Included among the surveyors were photographer James D. Hutton and naturalist Ferdinand Vandeveer Hayden. By early September, Bridger led Raynolds into the valley of the Bighorn River, based solely on his visit 34 years before, with General Ashley. The party wintered along the Oregon Trail, and by August of the same year, had reached the distant Fort Sarpy, built two decades before for the American Fur Company. Raynolds and Bridger found the fort in a state of "total confusion,"[79] apparently ignorant of the fact that the fur trade had long since ended. The presiding agent was far more interested in trading with the Indians than supplying a U.S. Army expedition on its way through unexplored country. To procure expedition essentials required obtaining them, almost at gunpoint, but Raynolds, at last, prevailed. Bridger's maps produced from the expedition were the only working maps used by the U.S. Army when war resumed between the government and the Sioux nation.

For a time, Bridger returned to work as a guide for commercial enterprises. In 1861, a group of Denver businessmen sought him out for advice on a Western railroad line across the Rocky Mountains to Salt Lake City, and points beyond. Such a project was not immediately practical, as the mountains west of Denver rise to a height of over 11,000 feet. Bridger accompanied Swiss-born surveyor Edward Berthoud on a journey into the mountains on May 10, 1861. According to Berthoud's notes, the 57-year-old Bridger knew the Rockies better than any man, living or dead, and that the pass they discovered had come by "the merest chance,"[80] within a two-minute walk. The report sent back to Denver recommended against a railroad through the pass, but Berthoud and Bridger's discovery opened up a major wagon train road that would eventually become Interstate 40, between Denver and Salt Lake City.

---

[78] Military, Raynolds Expedition – www.military.wikia.com/wiki/Raynolds_Expedition
[79] Military, Raynolds Expedition
[80] Elias Euler, Golden Cemetery Research Project, Edward Louis Berthoud – www.goldencemeteryblogspot.com/2008/08/captain-edward-louis-berthoud.html

Berthoud

A series of gold strikes in a different region caused a new stream of speculators to fill up routes west. The first strike of 1862 occurred in Bannock, Idaho. Virginia City's Alder Gulch followed in 1863, and gold was discovered in Last Chance Gulch soon thereafter. Already tense relations with the Arapaho, Cheyenne, and Sioux were exacerbated by the threat of a "swelling tide"[81] of prospectors. The new population soon swelled from a handful of white Americans to over 20,000. A more direct, southward route to the Virginia City region was sought from Wyoming, as new settlers were forced to trek around the Bozeman section of the Oregon Trail, southwest of modern-day Billings, Montana. Bridger found what would become the Bridger Trail as an alternative, creating it "from nothing."[82] He had traveled the country south of the Bozeman Trail years before in early reconnoitering missions. Colonel William O. Collins of the 11th Ohio Cavalry, Commander of the 6th Ohio, and Commander of Fort Laramie, heard of Bridger's past travels. The guide was contacted, and engaged to lead a group of settlers from Denver, through the Bighorn Basin, from Wyoming into Montana. He led Colonel Collins and his son, Lieutenant Caspar Collins, up the Sweetwater River and over the South Pass, around the west side of the Windy Mountains. The alternative route followed the Yellowstone and Shields Rivers, passing by the modern community of Wilsall, over the Bridger Mountains. A sub-range of the Rocky

---

[81] BigSkywords.com
[82] BigSkywords.com

Mountains, the Bridger Mountains cover a distance of approximately 40 miles, and reach 8,300 feet at their highest point.

In the spring of 1863, 10 wagon expeditions successfully passed through this newly-discovered route, two of them led by Bridger personally. Only then were Bridger's calculations transferred to ink and paper. He had included in his dirt etchings a perfectly detailed chart of all the "streams and watersheds,"[83] all of the old Indian trails alongside those carved by emigrants, and every "station"[84] along the way. The originals were given by Collins to John C. Friend over half a century later. Friend, in turn, donated them to the authors of *The Bozeman Trail*, Grace Raymond Hebard and Herbert E.A. Brininstool. Despite the rush to reach gold country, Bridger himself never contracted gold fever. Even though trapping had lost a good share of its market, he still preferred to traffic in beaver, which was still going for $8.00 per pound.

Between religion, gold, and a homesteading boom, the population grew to the point where the federal government felt compelled to create the Montana Territory. The Bozeman trail ran through the heart of it, and through the center of essential tribal hunting grounds, however, the alternative Bridger Trail did not. In 1864, an emigrant train departing from Denver traveled west of the Bighorn Mountains through the Bighorn Basin without the need of an escort. Leaving Laramie on May 20, the wagons went up the North Platte in a ten day, 140 mile trek to the Bridger Cutoff. Traveling west of Red Buttes, the group departed the main Oregon Trail, just west of present-day Casper, Wyoming, before heading southwest and skirting the Bighorn Mountains. In an itinerary that seems intricate on paper, but was extremely efficient compared to the traditional route, they crossed Badwater Creek, went up Bridger Creek into the area of the modern site of Lucerne, eight miles north of Thermopolis. From there, they forded the Greybull and Shoshone Rivers, and approached Montana by what is now Frannie, Wyoming. Finally, they went north to Clark's Fork on the Yellowstone River, and up to the area of Rock Creek, where the Bozeman Trail joins the Bridger, covering a total distance of 510 miles.

Bridger figured that if a wagon train made no major stops for prospecting, trapping, hunting, or fishing, the entire journey would be accomplished in 34 days. His own party took 50. So removed from civilization was the Bridger Trail that in the 21st century, the roads through the Bridger Mountains have remained unpaved.

Throughout 1864, Bridger continued to work at Fort Laramie for $10 per day, still holding the rank of Major. Not a standard foot soldier, and nearing 60 years of age, he was given leaves of absence for guiding emigrant trains to the Montana Territory.

Considering the danger to be courted on the Bozeman Trail, traffic on the Bridger Trail waned as discoveries of gold did the same. Eventually, it was all but abandoned as "things heated up"[85]

---

[83] Edmond S. Meaney, Review of The Bozeman Trail by Grace Raymond Hebard and E.A. Brininstool, the *Washington Historical Quarterly* Vol. 14, No. 1 (January 1923) p.68

[84] Edmond S. Meaney

along the Bozeman route. The First Powder River Expedition. with Bridger serving as guide, was launched against three tribes: the Lakota, Cheyenne, and Northern Arapaho. The Indian alliance had promised to close the Bozeman Trail and fight anyone who tried to cross it after a migration that had already seen 3,500 miners and settlers traverse the path. In what was to be known by some as Red Cloud's War, in honor of the Oglala Lakota Chief, the Indians had little choice but to stand firm, as their only source of food was being threatened. The U.S. Army had given the land to several tribes in the Fort Laramie area less than 20 years earlier, but were intent on saving a string of six forts along the route.

Red Cloud

A last diplomatic effort to stave off a war was under way, but a large force of cavalry, under the command of Colonel Henry Beebee, arrived at the most sensitive and inopportune time. Red Cloud saw the sudden appearance of 700 soldiers sent by General William Tecumseh Sherman as an invasion and broke off the talks. A companion of Red Cloud, Young Man Afraid of His Horses, threatened the American diplomats, telling them that "in two moons, you will not have a hoof left."[86]

In the wake of this, Bridger was engaged by Lieutenant Colonel Nathaniel Kinney to locate a suitable site for Fort C.F. Smith at a salary of $300 per month. He recalled that the construction efforts had suffered daily attacks by the Sioux. In a hurried attempt at informing the War Office

---

[85] BigSkywords.com
[86] Frederick J. Chiaventone, Jim Bridger

of what he rightfully believed was coming, Bridger sent the agency a letter warning that an Indian alliance would defend their section of the Bozeman Trail to their death, and that they had intended to attack all three forts simultaneously. His letter may have inspired some to send more soldiers, but in terms of federal caution, it was ignored.

In the hostilities that followed over the next two years, made up of mostly raids involving small numbers, Bridger served in an early action that destroyed an Arapaho village and helped to establish Fort Connor. This was thought to be enough to break the resolve of the Indians, but they were neither "defeated nor cowed,"[87] and they subsequently countered with added fury. One of the first battles of the Powder River conflict occurred on a December morning in 1866. Colonel Carrington held the highest rank at Ft. Kearney upon his arrival, but he wasn't a soldier with experience in battle. Rather, Carrington was a former lawyer with a background in design and engineering. Understanding his weakness in the face of an oncoming battle, he sought to offer leadership to one of his captains, William J. Fetterman, who outranked his colleague.

Carrington

---

[87] BigSkywords.com

Fetterman

A small-party attack came as Carrington returned to the fort with a wood train. Fetterman, who scoffed at the Indians' ability to fight, claimed that with 80 men, he could ride through the entire Sioux nation. That day, 80 men went out under his command and were slaughtered in the same kind of pursuit that would lead to disaster for George Custer at Little Bighorn. In the 40 minute battle, 40,000 arrows are thought to have been fired. In August of 1867, 500 Sioux were beaten back with the new Springfield breech-loading rifles, a much superior weaponry. In the Wagon Box attack, settlers and wood-cutters repulsed eight charges in under six hours. A quick-thinking Captain Powell circled 14 wagons behind which 24 enlisted men and six civilians fought for the better part of a day. Over 1,000 Sioux attacked under Red Cloud and High Back Bone, catching many soldiers outside of the camp who had to either fight alone or escape. The day ended when Major Benjamin Smith arrived with a howitzer in tow, causing the Indians to flee.

Over the following two years, the Indian alliance attained a string of victories, several in which Bridger participated. Illiterate as a young man, he later wrote brief accounts of those years. In the end, the U.S. Army withdrew and ceded the land once more under a new treaty. Of the Bozeman Trail forts, Fort Reno, Fort Kearney, and Fort C.F. Smith were abandoned to be burned to the ground by the Indian alliance.

In hindsight, some have wondered why the U.S. Army clung so fervently to its Bozeman Trail defenses when Bridger's new trail through the south was so efficient in terms of traveling time and safety. The route's creation was "no accident,"[88] as civilians used it to reach the gold deposits, but very few traversed the route in 1868, and it never gained substantial military support. That year marked end of Red Cloud's War, and Bridger again escorted army units to Yellowstone, having been recommended by the Chouteau Fur Company, with its longtime headquarters for mountaineers in what is now South Dakota.

Death and Legacy

Soon after the closing of the Bozeman Trail and the signing of the Fort Laramie Treaty, Bridger lost his officer's commission at Fort Laramie. Receiving his pay at Fort D.A. Russell near Cheyenne, he began to wander toward the east and home. With his explorer's instinct as sharp as it had ever been, his eyesight was nevertheless failing him, and the army could no longer find a way to compensate for his decreasing abilities. One biographer noted that James Felix Bridger would never have stayed in the East if he had full use of his eyes. Even at the end of his life, the author suggests Bridger could "still outtalk seven men."[89]

His eyesight almost gone, Bridger also became afflicted with severe rheumatism. At his farm near Kansas City in Westport, Missouri, a home he had procured for his family years before, his job was constrained to caring for the family's apple orchards. Still preferring the companionship of animals to people, he kept vigil with his horse, Ruff, and his dog, Old Sultan. Bridger died on the Westport farm on July 17, 1881. The U.S. government had, at last, paid his family for improvements made to the Ft. Bridger post, including 13 log structures and an 8-foot cobblestone wall, built, ironically, by the Mormons.

To reconstruct an accurate account of Bridger's travels and his influence on Western culture and politics, one must deal with scant evidence. There is little else but "old records to go on,"[90] and the memories of those who lived in his time have passed by two or three generations. Thomas L. Kearnes, in his review of J. Cecil Alter's tome on Bridger, reminds readers that the explorer kept no diary, wrote few letters, and in the most primitive medium available to him, "recorded much of his frontier business in the sand."[91] If Bridger himself did not leave a record of his thoughts, fair tribute can be found in the journals of others, such as the diaries of General William Ashley. His first employer took special pains to praise Bridger for his "unique abilities and reliability as part of a team."[92] He adds that Bridger would be "valued and trusted"[93] all his life. Ashley concludes by noting that while Bridger's life might not be explainable in a way that would "bring him great laurels,"[94] the mountain man had little interest in such things.

---

[88] James A. Lowe, WyoHistory.org, The Bridger Trail: A Safer Route to Montana Gold – www.wyohistory.org/encyclopedia/bridger-trail
[89] Famous Guide, Montana Historical Society, the Montana Magazine of History, Vol. 14 No. 3 (Summer, 1954) p. 63
[90] Stanley Vestal
[91] Thomas L. Kearnes
[92] FindaGrave.com, Jim Bridger – www.findagrave.com/cqi-bin/fq.cqi?page=gr&GRid=134
[93] FindaGrave.com
[94] FindaGrave.com

For its part, the Alter biography, despite being written close to the lifespan of its subject, sidesteps the inherent dangers of either glamorizing or taking up the prejudices of the day, and is still hailed as one of the best accounts on the life of Bridger, what one modern reviewer terms "a robust biography."[95]

Although Bridger concentrated in the land between the Dakotas and Idaho from the east to west, and between Montana and Utah from north to south, it is possible that he traveled as far south as Mesa Verde, as far north as the Yukon, and to the Pacific in the west. One scholarly account suspects he reached Great Slave Lake in Canada by "jest follerin the north star."[96] He allegedly reached the edge of the Arctic Ocean before reluctantly turning for home. In addition to the two major interstate highways that follow the routes Bridger discovered in the same century as Lewis and Clark's expedition, major railroads, two-lane highway systems, and communication routes were opened along the routes as well. In 1901, even the Bighorn Basin was developed for travel by the Chicago, Burlington, and Quincy Railroads.

Originally, Bridger was buried in an unmarked grave, but in 1904, his remains were relocated to Mt. Washington Cemetery in Independence, Missouri. Westport, a rural area in the 19th century, is now a neighborhood of Kansas City, boasting a statue of Bridger alongside Pony Express founder Alexander Majors and Kansas City founder John Calvin McCoy. A memorial inscribed on the Mount Washington monument simply reads, "James Bridger, 1804-1881, Celebrated as a Hunter, Trapper, Fur Trader, and Guide."[97]

---

[95] John A. Hogwood
[96] Norman B. Wiltsey
[97] Frederick J. Chiaventone

Thomas L. Beard's statue with Bridger on the right

The Bridger-Teton National Forest was established in 1931, and several other landmarks bearing his name can also be found throughout the modern West, many on major highway systems that came into being as a result of his expeditions. He is commemorated in many other large natural landmarks as well, such as in the Bridger Mountain Range of Montana, Bridger Park and Bridger Pass in south Wyoming, and in the Bridger National Forest.

In 1988, the gun Bridger carried through the western third of the nation for half a century found a home in the Museum of the Mountain Man after it had been sold at several auctions. A Hawken rifle from St. Louis, it was the only one he ever carried, and though it was his prized possession, he eventually sold the 34-inch, soft-barrel piece to Pierre Chien in 1865 for the sum of $65.

In the Oscar-nominated film *The Revenant*, Bridger's life as a teenager is depicted, but a wealth of material concerning his life remains to be covered by various artistic mediums. Meanwhile, books and documentaries on the most distinguished of the great explorers abound.

In the entire annals of the era of exploration in which Western routes through the Rocky

Mountains were opened, Bridger is believed to have possessed more knowledge about the land and the people who occupied it than any other living soul, including the Indians. As a fur trade frontiersman, scout, trapper, guide, merchant, army officer, and interpreter of multiple Indian dialects, his decades spent in the western third of the continent were "synonymous with the opening of the American west."[98] By staying past the end of the fur industry's height, he lived on as one of the last mountain men of the era in which the most persistent theme was "pioneer spirit."[99] Born before Lewis and Clark and growing up during the War of 1812, he saw the end of the Indian Wars in an expanding America, and he was acquainted with virtually every known figure in late 19th century history of the American West (even Father De Smet, a missionary to the Indians who traveled over 180,000 miles in his life's work). He knew George Armstrong Custer and was a friend of Sitting Bull, convincing him to participate in the Fort Laramie Treaty when no one else could. His name was known to all the great explorers of his time, including Kit Carson, Joe Meek, and the

Whitman family. William Henry Ashley may have been correct that Bridger's life is difficult to explain in a search for laurels, as no one would know precisely how to bestow them. However, those who knew him and studied his travels and associations might well agree that Bridger was "the epitome of his time, place, and chosen endeavor."[100]

Online Resources

Other books about the 19th century by Charles River Editors

Other books about Jim Bridger campaign on Amazon

Bibliography

A Brief History of the Beaver Trade – www.uscs.edu/Feinstein/A%20brief%20of%20beaver%20trade.html

A.L.C., Review of Stanley Vestal's Varied Life of Frontier Scout, Jim Bridger: Mountain Man: A Biography, Morrow, New York, *Southwest Review* Vol. 32 No. 2 (Sprin, 1947

Alter, Cecil J. Jim Bridger, University of Oklahoma Press, 1925, 9780-8061-1509-2

American West, Mountain Men, History on the Net – www.historyonthenet.com/American_West/mountain_men.htm

Big Sky Words.com, Montana's Mountain Men: Jim Bridger – www.bigskywords.com/montana-blog/mountains-mountain-men-jim-bridger

---

[98] Frederick J. Chiaventone
[99] Frederick J. Chiaventone
[100] Stanley Vestal

CDA Press.com, Jim Bridgeer – www.cdapress.com/colimeras/syd-albright/article_127eaa3a-Qea311e6.a1e3-1fe3-1f4d13cec7a5,html

Chiaventone, Frederick J., Jim Bridger, *Cowboys & Indians Magazine*

Despain, Matthew, Gown, Fred R., James Bridger, Utah History to Go, Utah History Encyclopedia – www.historytogo.utah.gov/people/jamesbridger.html

Despain , Matthew, Gowan, Fred R., James Bridger, *Utah Historical Quarterly*, - www.heritage.utah.gov/history/whg-people-bridger-james

Discovering Lewis & Clark, Warren's Lower Yellowstone – www.lewis-clark.org/article/1151

Doyle, Susan Badger, Journey to the Land of Gold: Emigrants on the Bozeman Trail, 1863-1866, *Montana: The Magazine of Western History*, Vol. 41 No. 4 (Autumn, 1991)

Encyclopaedia Britannica, Jim Bridger, Frontiersman – www.britannica.com/biography/Jim-Briger

Encyclopedia.com, James Bridger – www.encyclopedia.com/people/history/u-s-history-biographies/james-bridger

Everything, Jim Bridger – www.everything2.com/title/Jim+Bridger

Famous Guide, Montana Historical Society, the *Montana Magazine of History*, Vol. 4, No. 3, (Summer, 1954)

FindaGrave.com, Jim Bridger – www.findagrave.com/cqi-bin/fgicqi?page=gr&GRid=134

Fort Phil Kearney State Historic Site, Legends of America.com, Wyoming Indian Battles – www.legendsofamerica.com/wy-indianbattles5.html#Wagon-Box_Fight

Frank's Realm, Jim Bridger, Mountain Man – www.franksrealm.com/Indians/mountainman/pages/mountainman-jimbridger.htm

Gard, Wayne, Review of Cecil J. Alter's Rugged Mountain Men, *Southwest Review* Vol. 48 No. 3, Summer Fiction Special (Summer, 1963), Southern Methodist University

Gross, Chip, Jim Bridger, the 'Other" Mountain Man, NRA Family, Sept. 6, 2016

History.com, Jim Bridger – www.history.com/this-dday-in-history/jim-bridger-born

History.com, 1823, Ashley's Trappers Attacked by Indians – www.history.com/this-day-in-history/ahsleys-trappers-attacked-by-indians

History of Mormonism, 1857-1858, Utah War – www.historyofmormonism.com/mormon-history/utah_war_period/

Hughes, Michael, Dr., Native American Studies, High Plains Chatauqua- www.highplainschatauqua.org/jim-bridger.aspx

Jeff Arnold's West, Jim Bridger in Fact and Fiction – www.jeffarnoldsblogspot.com/2013/05/jim-bridger-in-fact-and-fiction.html

Karnes, Thomas L, Review of Cecil J. Alter's Jim Bridger, Arizona and the West, Vol. 6 No. 2 (Summer, 1964) *Journal of the Southwest*

Legends of America, Jim Bridger, Quintessential Guide of the Rocky Mountains – www.legendsofamerica.com/we=jimbridger.html

Linecamp.com, Jim Bridger – www.linecamp.om/museums/americanwest/western_names/bridger_jim/bridger_jim.html

Lowe, James A., The Bridger Trail: A Safer Route to Montana Gold – www.wyohistory.org/encyclopedia/bridger-trail

Meany, Edmond S., Review of the Bozeman Trail, Grace Raymond, Herbert E. A. Brinnistool, the *Washington Historical Quarterly*, Vol. 14, No. 1/January, 1923), University of Washington

Military Wiki, Raynolds Expedition – www.military.wikia.com/wiki/Raynolds_Expedition

Museum of the Mountain Men, Jim Bridger's Rifle, Sublette County Historical Society - www.museumofthemountainmen.com/jim-bridger-rifle/

National Park Service, Bighorn Canyon, Jim Bridger Floats the Bighorn – www.nps.gov/historyculture/jim-bridger-floats-the-bighorn.htm

Oregon Pioneers, Mary Ann Bridger, 1836-1848 – www.oregonpioneers.com/Mary/AnnBridger.htm

Oregon Spectator, March 23, 1848

Pierce, Ben, Outdoor Editor, Jim Bridger: The Man, the Myth, the Legend the Bozeman Chronicle, Jan. 28, 2016

Savages & Scoundrels, Jim Bridger – www.savagesandscoundrels.org/people/savages-scoundrels/jim-bridger/

Shooters Log, Tales of Survival: Hugh Glass, Mountain Man –

www.blog.cheaperthandirt.com/tales-survival-hugh-glass-mountain-man/

Spartacus Educational, James Bridger – www.spartacus-educational.com/WWBridgerJ.htm

Stillwell, Ted, Jim Bridger, Blanket Chief, The Examiner – www.examiner.net/news/20160817/ted-stillwell-jim-bridger-blanket-chief

The HistoryGlobe.com, The Oregon Trail – www.historyglobe.com/ot/ftbridger.htm

Utah Division of State History, John Weber – www.heritage.utah.gov/uhg-people-weber-john

Vestal, Stanley, Jim Bridger, Mountain Man; a Biography Quotes, Bookrags – www.bookdrop.com/studyguide-jim-bridger-mountain-man/quotes.htm1#95c.tab=0

Wiltser, Norman B., Jim Bridger, He-Coon of the Mountain Men, *Montana: The Magazine of Western History*, Vol. 6 no. 1 (Winter 1956)

Wyoming History.org, A Map of the West in His Head: Jim Bridger, Guide to Plains and Mountains – www.wyohistory.org/encyclopedia/jim-bridger

Wyoming Tales and Trails, Rendezvous – www.wyomingtalesandtrails.com/fur2.html

XRoads, University of Virginia, James Bridger, 1804 – www.xroads.virginia.edu/-hyper/hns/mtmen/jimbrid.html

Yellowstone Genealogy Forum J. Felix Bridger – Yellowstone Country, Feb. 18, 2004 – www.rootsweb.com/~mtygf/county/bridger-summary.htm

Made in the USA
Middletown, DE
16 September 2021